Honesty is for YOU and ME!

It pleases our God MOST definitely!

We PROMISE to tell the WHOLE TRUTH ...

1

When we try to hide
what we are doing inside,

we are allowing Satan to
make us do something we shouldn't do!

So YES!
His light shines through you and me
when we tell the truth wholeheartedly!

We did it on accident!
We are very sorry!

Let's do the right thing
and replace the vase.
Be proud of yourselves for your honesty
and know that His light shines
through us when we tell the truth!

5

And remember that it is better to give than to receive,

So, be kind and love one another
by always telling the truth to each other!

...to live with honesty and integrity
by telling the truth no matter who can see!

HONESTY and INTEGRITY!

11

for people all around the world,
but especially for YOU and ME!

About the Author

Kelly Kainer Billington was born and raised in Southeast Texas. She is a lovingly devoted wife, mother, and grandmother (Nana), and she advocates that her family and God are most important to her.

She earned her Bachelor of Science degree in Business Administration-Management w/Teacher Certification. After 12 years in public schools, she felt a calling to enter the real estate world. She became a broker, investor, and renovator and manages the family businesses.

She authors and creates her own website at www.kellykainerbillington.com. And she has included a beautiful tribute to her beloved Mother on her JOY Comes in the Morning web page. She created this page to honor her Mother whose middle name was JOY, and to honor her courageous battle with Alzheimer's. Kelly has written and copyrighted a documentary in regard to their experiences and discoveries of the Alzheimer's disease. She is sharing it on her website in hopes that it will help someone. She knows her Mother would be sporting that infamous MiMi smile if it were to help just one person! That is the kind of person she was! Simply Beautiful!

Kelly has written another children's book titled, God's Goodness in You and Me, which focuses on bringing God back to family life! She is also the author of the up and coming NANA and ME Series! This series focuses on topics like the Golden Rule, Honesty is the Best Policy, Cleanliness is next to Godliness, etc...

As Kelly continues to move forward in her career as an author, she hopes to help and inspire people of all ages with her publications!

WestBow Press books may be ordered through booksellers or by contacting:

WestBow Press
A Division of Thomas Nelson & Zondervan
1663 Liberty Drive
Bloomington, IN 47403
www.westbowpress.com
844-714-3454

Because of the dynamic nature of the Internet, any web addresses or links contained in this book may have changed since publication and may no longer be valid. The views expressed in this work are solely those of the author and do not necessarily reflect the views of the publisher, and the publisher hereby disclaims any responsibility for them.

Any people depicted in stock imagery provided by Getty Images are models, and such images are being used for illustrative purposes only.
Certain stock imagery © Getty Images.

Interior Image Credit: Daniel Majan

Scripture quotations taken from The Holy Bible, New International Version® NIV®
Copyright © 1973 1978 1984 2011 by Biblica, Inc. TM
Used by permission. All rights reserved worldwide.

ISBN: 978-1-6642-6045-0 (sc)
ISBN: 978-1-6642-6046-7 (e)

Library of Congress Control Number: 2022904591

Print information available on the last page.

WestBow Press rev. date: 09/12/2022

WESTBOW
PRESS®
A DIVISION OF THOMAS NELSON
& ZONDERVAN

Printed in the United States
by Baker & Taylor Publisher Services